AMERICAN PATRIOT
SPIRITUAL PATRIOT

Both being Requirements:
ONE NATION UNDER GOD

A Sequel to: Reclaiming National Sanity: Our Nation Under God

Prayer is the Key that Unlocks the Door to The Will of God
"Thy Will Be Done"

R. M. TROWBRIDGE, JR.

iUniverse, Inc.
Bloomington

American Patriot / Spiritual Patriot
Both being Requirements: ONE NATION UNDER GOD

iUniverse books may be ordered through booksellers or by contacting:

iUniverse
1663 Liberty Drive
Bloomington, IN 47403
www.iuniverse.com
1-800-Authors (1-800-288-4677)

ISBN: 978-1-4502-9918-3 (sc)
ISBN: 978-1-4502-9919-0 (ebk)

Printed in the United States of America

iUniverse rev. date: 03/15/2011

FORWORD

A Sequel to Reclaiming National Sanity: Our Nation Under God

Conversation

An individual named Origen observed that the soul is frozen spirit and by extension of the analogy, the body is frozen soul, and that idea is of something utterly real, though immaterial, manifesting through increasing densities, ending in a temporary body of materiality. The body's very solidity is a result of its animation by the soul. When the soul leaves the body – what we call death – the body dissolves away.

The lower principles (laws) have their form and existence only because of the higher principles (laws), and this crucial proposition is not acceptable or congenial to the contemporary (modern) mind. Men in ancient times and our founders had the intelligence to see that man is body, soul, and spirit; and that spirit is primary (one part body and two parts spirit). Thus we have a firm reliance on Devine Providence. And thusly so, the Constitution came into being. Now, in our modern age, we have come to believe (act) and think that man is merely body with a bit of mind added. This is the root problem. Our founders having the intelligence to recognize that we are body, soul, and spirit – One part body (33 1/3 %) – two parts spirit (66 2/3 %), and that when the government restrains the people, then the spirit is restrained.

When this spiritual malady is overcome, we will straighten out mentally and physically, individually and collectively as a Nation.

Life is an intelligence test. Failure in life is always a failure in intelligence. The intelligent man can <u>hold</u> to what is good for him, because intelligence is precisely the ability to discriminate between right and wrong and the power (grace) to choose the right. Success has as many definitions as there are individuals. Failure has only one definition, the inability to succeed--- choosing the right.

Our founders, being Christian men with Christian values, chose God centered, Christ centered laws for each child of the Republic to incorporate into their lives, giving others an opportunity for the same practice should they choose to do so. Thusly, ONE NATION UNDER GOD. These men were spiritually awake. Thusly they could be declared as American Patriots and Spiritual Patriots rolled up into one entity, individually and as a collective through which gave us The Constitution.

What does "awakening" refer to? You know, the awakening of a sleeping giant. Awakening refers to getting back to our Source, "Under God". Spiritually dead would be those like atheists, meaning those who believe (act) that there is no power greater than themselves. Spiritually asleep would be those like agnostics who have not lost their faith, and have not sunk, and are not stuck in deliberate and enjoyable evil acts, who practice their religion seriously and try hard to live right, but have only a mental and theoretical knowledge of God that is dry, and for most of them, reading the Good Book is like chewing a mouth full of sawdust and trying to swallow it. Therefore it is not alive for them as a reader. This would be where it was said "Question with boldness the very Existence of God" as stated by one of our nations' founders would come into play. This would be The Practical Life (common since) Means Practice. ["There is a principle which is a bar against all information, which is proof against all arguments and which cannot fail to keep a man in everlasting ignorance – that principle is contempt prior to investigation" H. Spencer.] Investigation here means to practice the principles and observe the results of that practice which will convince the practitioner of their validity or, if you will, the very existence of God.

If you are *Spiritually awake,* you see and *know* God directly, as directly as you know the air you breath, the food you eat, and the earth underneath your feet. One actually sees the Presence of God (His essence) in all things which is the Art of Prayer or Prayer without Ceasing. The Eye on top of the pyramid on our One Dollar Bill currency is the spiritual eye of the soul, which *knows* its kinship to Our Creator, endowed to each of us by our Creator, granting spiritual freedom in union with our physical bodies granting physical freedom as well. There is obviously a union between the soul and the body, thusly the sacred union of the soul with the body. Consider the marriage vow of "until death do us part." Today, we are not really devoted to each other, which have been exemplified by our lack of honor and devotion one to another, a lack of *humility*.

The Practical Life means Practice.

Practice What? How about those God Centered, Christ Centered (Laws).

Remember that we are a nation respective of *laws, not of men*.

Plato stated "One of the penalties of not participating in politics is that you will be governed by your inferiors". That would be Take-over by occupation.

Laziness is the neuroses eating away at the fabric of our existence and our national well being and existence.

What *laws*? How about the Absolutes listed below?

Absolute honesty: No lying, no cheating, no stealing, in all your affairs. Simply put, absolutely no falsehoods.

Absolute purity: Purity of mind, purity of body, purity of emotions, purity of heart, and sexual purity.

Absolute unselfishness: Seeking what is right and true in every situation, above what you want.

Absolute love: Loving God with all your heart, all your soul, all your mind, and all your strength, and loving your neighbor as yourself.

Principles are <u>laws that</u> govern. (I explained this in my other book Reclaiming National Sanity: Our Nation Under God).

None of the above *laws* choose a person.

None of the above *laws* remember you.

<u>*You*</u> have to remember them and <u>*you*</u> have to choose the *laws.*

Remember the saying: "Many are called and few are chosen."

If <u>*you*</u> choose to practice the laws daily, then <u>*you*</u> are chosen.

The afore mentioned Four Absolutes are the yardstick by which spiritual progress is measured and the *virtues* that are developed interiorly, manifesting physically, giving a man or a woman their character based on principles, or laws endowed by our Creator. God doesn't call the qualified; He qualifies the called by their choices.

The *Spiritual* life is not a theory. No, we have to live it.

The grace (power) of the New Testament is hidden (occult) *in* the letter of the Old or *THE LAW.* That is why St. Paul says that "the *law* is spiritual". Thus the letter of the law, superseded, grows old and decays, while its spirit, perpetually renewed, stays young. For grace (power) is altogether immune to decay. The *Law* checks the actualization of evil. This (the law vs. grace) would be what Christ was referring to when He said "the first shall be last and the last shall be first". He was <u>not</u> referring to any sect, or specific group of individuals, race, color, or creed, or any particular religious persuasion. He – Christ – knew that because we did not believe (i.e., practice the Laws given to Moses), then we would not believe Him either, even though He was the fulfillment of The Laws, made manifest (i.e., Absolute honesty, purity, unselfishness, and love), thereby sanctifying us all. However, we <u>*must*</u> choose. This is also why He said "Follow me": Ancient yet Modern. Remember, He still lives.

The word occult (adj.) used above simply means hidden from view; concealed.

Paul, prior to receiving guidance from Christ (a blast off the Hot Wire from the Absolute), executed his job with proficiency, which when he (Paul) would ask if you were a Christian, and you replied with a "yes", he would offer to hold your coat, and after you gave it to him, he would cut off your head with his sword. That was his job. That was the real Paul. Then the blast off the Hot Wire came which knocked him off his horse or donkey (I was not there so I don't know which animal it was) asking "Why persecuteth thou me?" This spiritual experience (blast off the hot wire) left him totally blind for five years, which he then could not relate to, and had to be helped by those Christians whom he would have beheaded before. Obviously, you do not want such a powerful message to begin your conversion with God. You may want one like that received by a man named Bill Wilson whose experience was much gentler; however, both men thought they had gone nuts because neither of them could relate to something higher than themselves. You want an educational variety type spiritual conversion experience by doing your homework which is just as valid, and produced by practicing the four absolutes in all your affairs as best you can. Washington had his vision (mentioned in *Reclaiming National Sanity: Our Nation Under God:*) which was given him, by grace, however, he was already a believer (by his actions) and it was not a jolt to his psyche or soul. We are now in the third phase of the Vision given him by (as he said) the lady in blue who first called him "Son of The Republic" and said to George "Look and Learn", then an Angel with "UNION" embedded in its brow showed him things and George saw a hoard of Angels of Light backing up this Angel awaiting commands. Later, when he had come back to himself, he told one of his friends that he had often wondered what death would be like.

How about the old hymn of "Onward Christian Soldier" that I remember from my childhood? I chose a Michael Jackson's "Thriller" or a Janis Joplin's "Me and Bobby McGee," songs by artists - irresponsibly going down the road, windshield wipers slapping time in my youth, theirs ending in death via drug overdose. Could this be considered a diva centered life style of living? You decide. Or, perhaps you venture out with your "friends" for a party after taking some pill of some kind like LSD, or ICE, or some chemical of some kind, (I'm not talking about good Rx drugs here that are good), then the food on your plate begins to wiggle, or the floor begins to become wavy and won't stay still either, and the others around you are not experiencing the same phenomenon, or you're in a room with others and you begin seeing and talking to "something", but the friends next to you are not seeing or hearing it, while it's perched on the mantle you are pointing to, wanting "it" to stop and now you are getting paranoid, so you get up, change positions hoping it will stop, but "it" doesn't.(Remember, it's not over, until the Gorilla (the drug) says it's over, but you don't know this). Finally, coming back to yourself after the phenomenon has ceased, and not dying during this experience, which was real to you but no one else around you experienced it, and you again ask your "friend" "did you see that?" and they replied, "You're Nuts" or "Cool" depending on their position. Or you may go to some pricey psychologist and share, who tells you that was just a hallucination, not real. You may omit your use of drugs, which opened a door or window intended to remain closed while we are in this life. Unknown to you and possibly him, the door to the other side, which your soul just witnessed that became intelligible to your brain, was opened temporally from which you returned safely, by grace. You now return home keeping your mouth shut and knowing you would rather do jail time than let your parents, priest, or minister know what had actually happened. These are spiritual experiences, but ones of the wrong kind, leaving behind paranoia, confusion, a lack of peace, frustrations, and miseries. No one should enter into these areas without permission from God.

By the way, Hitler's drug of choice was peyote. I wonder which set of entities, the higher or lower principalities, were influencing his mental processes or thinking? You get three guesses and the first two don't count.

Today, our national drug of choice is money and/or some kind of chemical drug to get high on. When we don't get our way, we are depressed, and when we do get our way, we are euphoric. It might be well to remember that benevolence is cumbersome and is a form of interfering self righteousness that pursue the ideas of scheming and getting, where education has failed because of unchecked ambition, therefore interfering with brotherhood. It is better to hold fast to the intuitive good that promotes brotherhood.

This reminds me of Wyle coyote of Disney fame, coming up with all his imagined great ideas to capture the illusive roadrunner, all of which kept blowing up on him. In our case, the governing, coming up with all their great ideas that keep blowing up affect more than just them.

Today, a lot of our youth apparently have difficulties squaring up a hat on their head, much less squaring up their lives, like paying the rent on time, taking care of their off spring, et. al., but they seem to think they can enter success through a window, by drug usage, and manage or control what is going on over there, where there are no door handles, furniture, solid rear ends to deal with, then return to where doors are solid, furniture is solid, rear ends are solid, and manage their lives when everything about them is declaring their unmanageability, even their sane friends telling them so, calling manure... manure and a rose... a rose not confusing the fragrances, like that Ms

S.E. Cupp gal on the Fox network, calling some guy a dirt bag (a piece of s---), which he was being a dirt bag. Guys, don't let the skin fool you, I'm pretty sure she is kind, gentle, fun to be around, loving, and understanding, however, should you begin behaving unworthily, she can be rougher than the back tire on a four-wheeler. Those in their thirties or forties plus years, may have dispensed with drug usages, or they may never have used drugs at all, wearing 3 piece suits, and still cannot balance a check book or even a federal check book, holding meetings, having discussions, sharing their points of view to resolve something with nothing resolved at the end of the meeting. This reminds me of group conscience meetings at Losers Lounge, lots of discussions, no results. These three piece suit individuals calling themselves winners? Opinions are worthless; Experience is priceless, ever reminding us to place principles *before* personalities.

Could it be that our Creator could have been unaware of the influence of drugs in our culture and might not have addressed this, a dilemma that, is now staring us in the face? I think not. In fact, He did address this issue, however his address was mistranslated in the King James version which was completed in 1611. The translators were not solely working with the Greek but also drew upon earlier translations, and chief among these was the Vulgate, a translation from the Greek into Latin finished by St. Jerome in AD 404. *Pharmakeia* in the original Greek New Testament was rendered as *venefica* in the Latin Vulgate and then as *"sorcery"* in the King James Version. A look at the definitions of these three words indicates an interesting pattern: *Pharmakeia* has three meanings; *veneficia* retains only two of these; "sorcery" retains only one of the original three, and that in a less specific sense than either the Latin or Greek. *Pharmakeia* means drugging, poisoning, or sorcery. *Venefica* loses the specific, root reference to drugging – a crucial loss. Check out Galatians 5:19-21 and substitute the word drugging for the word witchcraft (sorcery); Revelations 9:20-21 substitute the word druggings for the word sorceries. Then do the same for; Revelations 18:21-23; Revelations 21: 7-8, Revelations 22:11-15: Webster defines sorcery as "the use of power gained from the assistance or control of evil spirits." Both *pharmakeia* and *venegicium* apply specifically to a drug-related use of power coming from evil spirits. Lucifer is real enough, and did he ever find a loop hole to hammer us with. He and his minions have had millennia of experience finding weaknesses to use to his advantage to influence our decisions. He even tried to influence the Absolute while he was here. We can't just discard or blow him off, and we can't cast him out. We really do need a power greater than ourselves to help us. Lucifer's purpose is getting us to wake up and *choose sides*. Just look around and witness what is going on, what we are so caught up in and what we are worshiping in some of our practices. The Good Book refers to Lucifer a lot, and it talks about spirits a lot. But we can ask for God's protection and care with complete abandon, yielding to His Divine Providence, while practicing honesty, purity, unselfishness, and love, to the best of our abilities, and not selling them out in our deeds, words, or thoughts. Man moves by a thought, word, then deed process or direction – while God moves by a deed, then word, then thought process or direction; Thus the, act your way into right thinking process – the doing of the next right thing. This is why practice these principles (honesty, purity, unselfishness, love) in all our affairs, which changes our words and our thinking which allows us to live from our higher selves, our God given self which now influences our thinking.

When a man or woman takes a jigger of spirits, now coming under the influences of the spirits, beginning to act more unworthily if consuming too many jiggers – like the man who takes a drink, then the drink takes another drink (jigger), then the drink takes the man. Now the man or woman is no longer under the influence of the Spirit of God (although still present), but quite the contrary, under the influence of the spirits and looking for Mister Smith and Wesson for whatever reason. Would it not be better to swallow a jigger of truth (honesty) and dispense a cup of kindness, being under the influence of the Spirit of God – You decide.

Ask yourself the following question: Could your betrayal of the absolute law have anything to do with getting the girl intoxicated, stupefying her conscience to the point where she does not have the ability to say no while her britches are coming down, so that some dirt bag can now drive his truck into her now unguarded pasture gate, dumping his load and leaving behind physical and emotional scars, with no regard to whether there will be a crop or not? Women are sacred and special, all women. If they choose to lower their values, their dignity, their integrity, that's their call. Sex comes from the root word "sacrum" which means sacred. Such a union should be loving, joyful, and sacred. So, ladies, it might be wise and to your advantage to learn to keep your legs crossed, controlling yourself, no matter how shiny or good looking the truck, otherwise your loyalty could become as that of a country dog – the first one to feed ya - gets ya, thereby allowing yourself to become someone's common place pole scratcher. It's your honesty being dealt with here in either case. How many ways do you want to self justify your choice, or lay blame on others. When misconduct or behaving unworthily is present, then self justification kicks in, which is a form of dishonesty to one's self or lying to one's self, and denial sets in. This is where spiritual guts need to be grown, based on principles, thereby the growing a conscience as well. Conscience must be grown, which is weak but present at birth within our instincts. Principle adherence by use of the will and attention develops conscience and spiritual guts coupled with prayer.

By the way, did you know that when you remove water from the chemical formula for alcohol (CH_3CH_2OH), what remains is the chemical formula for ether? Should we ingest too much alcohol at a party or where-ever and eventually relieve ourselves, essentially getting rid of the water, we should then be filled with ether, which was used as a prep for surgery of some kind before today's modern preps. Then couldn't we expect the removal of some things from our lives, like wives, homes, cars, bank accounts, relationships, children, proportional thinking, or even body parts? Are we so drugged that we do not care anymore? Nothing is wrong with alcohol when it is used properly. Each person has to decide what too much is for them. Too much leads to DTs or death! DTs being funny figures you are seeing and addressing that no one else is seeing. Now we have stronger drugs, too. It would be wise to note that one cannot experience something that does not exist. George Washington and our other founders did not have drugging problems to do battle with, we do. George did briefly visit the higher entities by grace, while we visit the lower entities by drugging, both of which are intelligible (perceivable) by the soul, not the flesh. Did you know that *distilled spirits* were introduced into England only in the second half of the sixteenth century; the distilling process (invented in Islam in the 9th century) becoming practical on a commercial scale elsewhere in Europe only in the fifteenth century.

In my elementary school in the early 1950's, schools handed out paper book covers to protect the text books and issued stamps (like postage stamps) to decorate the covers with. One stamp that I remembered, but ignored later in life which was my ignorance, had a bottle (a fifth) of alcohol with a skull and cross bones (in white) across it and the word poison (in red) on the bottom of the stamp. Another stamp had the grim reaper on it and the words don't drink and drive. Symbols were used as warnings to communicate to the youth long before drinking or driving would have arrived into their living experiences. Today, it appears to me that our society promotes poisonings of one kind or another, declaring it to be "cool" for whoever's profitable gain. You choose, or you decide.

It does not take a Harvard degree to figure out what is happening. Simply observe how far down the scale we have degenerated by way of our practices. We really need to grow some stronger spiritual guts, which I will address a little later on. Our country is a battle ground within a playground, to be taken seriously but not too serious.

Simply ask some of our youth who have experimented with drugs or old-timers who experimented with alcohol. Why do we fail to experiment with finding God?

Could this have anything to do with Spiritual in its nature, moral in its humanity, or Spiritual in its nature, immoral in its humanity? It most certainly does in my view.

Could this be considered thinking outside the box?

Let me state here and now that I am not against the use of alcohol or drugs at all, when applied or used properly. They too are a gift. I am grateful for them in more ways than you could imagine.

Don't take my words for any more than that. Do your own homework. There are many smarter and greater men than me, all of whom have been provided by our Creator.

This is why we are a nation respective of *laws* (spiritual in their nature, moral in their humanity), not of men. Our nation has the power (grace) to renew its-self in accordance with the *law*. This applies to individuals, and to the national collective. We must return to the practice of the four 4 Absolutes, (honesty, purity, unselfishness and love), thereby checking the actualization of evil, (i.e. the deliberate, voluntary, enjoyment and love of the practice of evil; dishonesty, impurity, selfishness, unlovingness (anger, hate, resentments). Clearly, someone wise, or a nation being wise, *abandons* what is corruptible (temporal) and *unites* its whole being to what is incorruptible (eternal and immortal). Just consider the wording of the United States of America or One Nation under God or the "In order to form a more perfect Union".

Remember, our country, the United States of America is "One Nation under God" indivisible. Therefore, *it is God alone who is our own and we offer our hearts and our lives to him so that He may bestow his compassion upon us, and reveal his presence to us.*

So, the Will of God (honesty, purity, unselfishness, love) will never take us to where the Grace of God will not protect us. Therefore, the task ahead of us is <u>never</u> as great as the Power behind us.

You know, the, *you* will intuitively and instinctually know how to handle situations which use to baffle us.

You can never be too stupid to get it, however, you can be to smart (intelligent) to get it. Degreed intelligence (knowledge) is good and used for earning a living, however, it is not the final word. The, you will know it in your gut is more reliable than degreed knowledge (i.e. degreed intelligence). The more the degreed knowledge filling the mind only succeeds in emptying the heart, bringing a far less regard for the people. When armies go to war, *sorrow* is the only victor, and the war between the mind and the heart is not unlike any other physical war, should the intellect prevail over the heart, *sorrow* for the people ensues, for the spirit no longer prevails.

Our government has many highly degreed individuals, and look where we are now. The more poverty stricken the people, the sharper the weapons of enforcement; the deeper the common misery, the more police and soldiers, the less rewarded the laborer; the more numerous the laws, the more thieves and robbers. Therefore, the wisest of leader will trust God and adopt a policy of "let alone". One should rule a great country as you fry a small fish, with the least turning. The riches of contentment are most easily gained where ruling begins in self-government by the individual. Learn to govern yourself first.

None of the material within these pages are original thoughts of my own. I have only come to realize the truths conveyed by practicing of the Absolutes as closely as humanly possible (which have been sporadic but persistent with efforts over the past 38 years).

Remember the saying: "The Way is narrow" or "many are called, few are chosen".

I say the chosen are the ones who choose. Our founding fathers chose. The, "if you can keep it" saying by Franklin.

Choose What?

Choose "The Way"!

Remember, materialistic illusions will not get us there. There being national sanity and recovery.

"The Way" is the <u>Exit Ramp</u> between the cities of Sodom and Gomorra where selfishness, self centeredness, and self will ran riot.

Following "The Way" is following the God centered, Christ centered laws [Christ], who showed men how to live, and is like going hunting with a Game Warden; just because you see it does not mean you can take it, unless you whip and cut the Game Warden, and this is only dealing with hunting rules; in living our lives by the rules (honesty, purity, unselfishness, love) as best we can, we are going to be ok – unless we whip and cut the Absolute (Christ). Ancient yet Modern. Remember, He said He was always with us; the living principles – *alive* - of which we are all a part of. The *spiritual life* is not a theory – we have to live it.

What is "The Way"? Consider a passage from the 24 Magazine, June 1973 issue: "*The Way is so big you have to struggle to hang on to its meaning from day to day. You will need all the strength you have merely to remember it, not because it is dim or remote but on the contrary because it is immediate, relevant, true, and beautiful beyond our hopes.*

The Way is a method, a program, a means, and a power for achieving a definite result: a radical change (metanoia) in human consciousness and human nature, bringing with it freedom from want and fear, regeneration of the whole person, and the true brotherhood of man. It's no small thing, but small and weak people can do it, indeed are peculiarly qualified to do it. The Way is not a religion, but all real religion springs from it – not a science, but all real science obeys its principles – not an art, but all real art is a communication of it. The Way is the power which keeps the stars in their courses, and shows men how to live. It is the way the universe works, and the way *you* work when you are in your right mind. It is the Norm of human life. People are sane when they obey it, and insane when they ignore it. The Way is what the rationalists call the *First Principles of Practical Reason* and the faithful call it *The Kingdom of Heaven*. All things are made by it, supported by it, and received by it at death. The Way is the Life (Zoe). It is the Law (Torah) and the Presence (Shekinah), the Road (Tariqa) and the Struggle (Akbar), the Path (Tao) and it's Power (Teh), the Pattern (Rita) and the Method (Dharma). It is Logos-Sophia, Atman, the ruling Power of the universe in its aspect of illuminator and guide to the human race. It is the TRUTH, the ultimate Reality, the Self-existent, the Suchness-Aletheia, Sat, al Haqq, Aehyeh, Tathata. It is Christ, God himself as teacher, helper, friend, and savior of men. It is the King of kings and the Lord of lords, the blessed and only Potentate. It is all this at one and the same time. And whether you like it or not, or believe it or not, you are dealing with it – positively or negatively – every hour of your life."

To me, this is the True top down, bottom up (the small and weak who are indeed peculiarly qualified to do it) and inside out; the Tea Party Movement – which can become very high, deep and special; not the Van Jones thing – which is very common, vulgar, in fact inescapable, and definitely not a prince for peace, but a prince for chaos whose riding companions are the Four Horsemen of

Conquest, War, Famine, and Death, and he (Van) knows it not. I really do hope that he (Van) wakes up soon and I wish him no malice.

Christ, or if you will, God made manifest in living flesh, did not promote the death of humans and stated no man wants to die and neither did he want to die, however He was willing to do so for the deliverance or salvation of the whole and all of mankind. His death has been twisted by the spiritual leaders of other nations promoting dying as a good thing for their causes, whatever their purposes which promote their egotistical arrogant aspirations (false light). Christ stated that unless a seed of corn fall to the ground and die, it cannot bring forth good fruit. The death of the seed is referring to the dying unto ourselves, our selfishness and self centeredness produced by our ego self, which stands in the way of our usefulness to others and our fellow man. He was referring to ego reduction, not the taking of human life. Remember, God is Life. Our nation promotes life, not the destruction of lives. Many folks want to serve God, but only as advisors, because it is easier to preach ten sermons than it is to live one, which is what I call preachercraft or parrot talk.

It blew me away too. I had no idea. It's time to *wake up.*

There are four degrees of Christian men's living beholding to the course and manner of their calling, and they are Common, Special, Singular, and Perfect. Three of these begin and end in this life, and the fourth may by His grace (power) begin here and shall become everlasting without end in the bliss of Heaven which exists simultaneously in time. To me that represents "in order to form a more perfect union" – namely our Constitution.

This is really high octane stuff and difficult to burn especially within my unprepared brain (intellect). The soul already knows this; it just has real difficulties in communicating this information to our brain but our instincts sense the truth. The brain is an instrument of the Soul. If you think otherwise, simply ask any corps on its way to the marble orchard (grave yard), seeing yourself of course, and asking; What is missing within you that no longer sees, smells, feels, speaks (you know, the wagging of your tongue), or tastes, or loves? Oh, I forgot, the Soul is no longer present, giving life to the body in the Presence of our Creator, who keeps the Heart beating and the blood flowing in our veins. Therefore, you the departed cannot tell me. I have to figure it out for myself, discover it for myself, and then attempt to communicate it to others while being rejected by others.

Don't let the high octane stuff put you off.

You may already be actively involved in The Way and not know it; if you seek the good and serve it, and if you are trying however humbly to be a real decent human being, then you are on The Way. Whether you can <u>stay</u> on it, and <u>succeed</u> on it depends on your fidelity (devotion) and fortitude (guts) to live your life that way without quitting or selling out.

Here the word guts means *Spiritual* guts which must be grown. No one is born with this set of guts. These guts or strengths are developed by the practice of *Spiritual* principles. The principles of honesty, purity, unselfishness, and love, are the only negotiable currency for the day. Principles are the higher currencies; whereas monies (dollars) are lower currencies. One is not to place low values in high places. At birth our guts are the norm for human life, needing food to begin with and then later on some money, some power, some position to earn a living, and reproduction (sex) to live a fulfilling happy life. Spiritual guts are those guts (virtues or principals- honesty, purity, unselfishness and love) that cannot be purchased by the offerings of the kingdoms of the world, the riches of the world, the highest positions of the world, or even food of which all of these were offered the Absolute (Christ) while he was in the desert, refusing all the kingdoms, wealth (money), women, and even food when being tempted to turn the rocks into bread when He was hungry because He had the power to do it. Just look at the Egyptian in Cairo who refused the offerings of money and food and would not sell out his brothers and sisters and add to the violence and chaos. That sure looks like the actions of a Christian to me even if he may not recognize it at this time for himself. Congratulations Egypt! Now the question is the following: Which spirit will you choose to follow? Those individuals whose riding companions are the Four Horsemen of Conquest, War, Famine, and Death of which are reflected in the Ancient Egyptian Book of the Living, which takes life away from the common man because of the serving of self interests of selfishness and self centeredness which is ego based, or will you choose the Ancient Egyptian Book of the Dead, which gives life following Osiris and Pymander (which is Christ prior to his coming) of your Ancient world, which the collective voluntarily served which built one of the greatest cultures of the ancient world and served the people before the corrupt leaders came into power to get the monies (gold), power, and positions for themselves leaving the common man to be walked on. I'll bet the youth of Egypt do and did not know that. It's not religious, it's spiritual. Today it is Christ (the Absolute) because He came unto His own.

The <u>truth</u> (honesty) shall set you free.

What does the <u>truth</u> (honesty) first succeed in doing?

It <u>offends</u>. Thus, the discomfort, the offense to my ego personality, leaves me in a blaming state and much discomfort because of the denial of my state (my actions) of unworthiness. I have not been behaving worthily with regards to honesty, purity, unselfishness, or love and knew it not, given my situation.

Remember the saying in the Good Book "I have come not to appease but to offend." This is where we start looking for some wood, a few nails, and a high hill to crucify the fulfillment of Absolute honesty, Absolute purity, Absolute unselfishness, and Absolute love (who came unto his own and his own received him not) [Ancient yet Modern] and instead, we choose to set free the thieves and murderers and place low values in high places, therefore ourselves behaving unworthily with regards to our kinship to Our Creator.

As American Patriots as well as Spiritual Patriots rolled up into one entity, we are the defenders (warriors) responsible for defending and practicing, both as individuals and as a Nation. Remember when the Absolute, in living flesh, - Christ – stated to Pilate that "you have only that power over me which is given to you from above" then stated "My Kingdom is not of this world and there are those who would see that I would not be taken". The Absolute, The Exemplar of the foundation of our One Nation under God; The Executive and Sovereign Monarch of our One Nation under God, and the Universe. It is the truth.

The universe is tapping us on the shoulders, attempting to awaken us, and trying to inform our intellects (brains) to clean up our own house, while we defend our rights and the rights of others which have been endowed by our Creator to see that We The People, and Our Nation, are not taken. The Tea Party movement attempting to get us back to practicing principles before personalities.

In my previous book Reclaiming National Sanity: Our Nation Under God, I mentioned the axiom "not doing is doing". I think Franklin said the same thing when he said, "a penny saved *is* a penny earned".

Our Nation sure seems to be an offense to other nations.

Because we the people attempt, however humbly, to live in accordance with the *laws*, other nations seek our demise. Remember that this is "One Nation under God,"- indivisible.

Remember the saying in the Good Book "I *am* that light that lighteth each man that cometh into the world" or "without me, you can do nothing." Maybe we as individuals and as a Nation really do have a kinship and responsibility for allegiance to our Creator. This is where the "I in thee and thou in me" come into play or into my being or our national being.

It appears the religious people have it right. Prayer is the key that unlocks the door to the Will of God. We simply need ask for knowledge of His Will and the power (grace) to carry it out *daily*. Then we're covered. He's got our backs.

When I recognized my own unworthiness I used the following prayers before beginning my request for knowledge of His Will. Ancient yet modern, and a prayer used by an individual who obviously knows *how to pray*. There are other prayers, however this is the one I chose. Personally, I did not know how to pray, however, I did know how to prey. Boy, was I confused. It's *your* honesty being dealt with here.

The prayer I chose or rather that was given to me by my mentor came from Matthew:

"Lord, I am unworthy that thou should come under my roof, but speak the word only and thy servant shall be healed." I would repeat this three times.

Next (beginning with my own unbelief rather than belief –doubt that anything was there listening- and I grew up attending The First Christian Church) the Agnostic part of myself, insincere and not really hopeful, but willing to perform the experiment. Willingness here was the Key, not perfection or belief.

The Prayer: "Lord, I know thee to be a generous and magnificent Prince, as Powerful as thou art good; I therefore give myself to thee without reserve; I wish to serve thee without knowing what I am to gain by it each day or year or even at the end of my career. I promise to think of nothing but your interests, and, as for my own, I abandon them entirely to your discretion or rather to your goodness and liberality." - - - J.P. de Caussade, S.J.

Then I would say: "I do not know what is to happen to me today, weather troublesome things or pleasant ones, whether I shall be happy or sad, in consolation or in grief, but it will all be as you please and I abandon myself to your providence and I submit to all your wishes."

Lastly, I would close my prayer time with the following:

"Lord Jesus Christ, son of the Living God, Have Mercy on Me."

I was told to start with only 10 minutes of prayer time first thing in the mornings and that anyone can do 10 minutes. No one can lie their way around this practice.

How was I to know if the experiment was working? By a feeling of relief and peace, followed by a positive change in the way your life goes and it is a relief and a change you can, and should, feel every day of your life.

In the beginning I did not know what the word Mercy meant, honestly I could have cared less. Again, I had a misunderstanding of what that word meant. When I was thirty years old, mercy had a Janis Joplin meaning: "Lord won't you buy me a Mercedes Benz, my friends all drive Porches, I must make amends". She died of a heroin overdose. Today I know the spiritual meaning of the word mercy – <u>jump into my skin.</u>

He enters into our hearts and minds in a manner that is indeed miraculous.

Ah, the afore mentioned come under my roof thing. Go figure.

What came to meet me as a result of this daily practice was a conversion experience characterized primarily by altered response in which quiet and serenity predominate . . . .associated with that altered response are other changes like the loss of automatic hostility; the disappearance of the perfectionistic drive; the disappearance of the egocentric power drive; the appearance of a better response to work demands; and finally, the appearance of a much greater capacity for objectivity. Other changes in attitude accompany the new state . . . The new feelings which appear are distinctly spiritual in quality and alter the psychic picture in the direction of what it must be conceded are healthier reactions.

On some occasions my mentors would increase the strength of my medications from 100 prayers (mg) to 500 prayers (mg) for 30 days only. The prayer I used was my closing prayer, repeated repetitively in rhythm with my normal breathing pattern.

Once again, my mentor was right. He said "when you bend your knee, it is an outward expression of an inward desire. And something inside *you* (the resistance) begins to break down, and you can begin to receive something higher". He also said "Nothing turns our Creator into a bigger marsh-mallow than honesty when approached, especially the admittance of unknowing so that we begin to <u>know</u>, for He is a generous giver, and has all the power to boot." He also said the following:

"When you approach Him, when kneeling, keep your back straight with your head gently bowed keeping your arrogance in check. Our Creator does not want a limp dishrag full of self pity, sitting or standing or kneeling there. This is sacred time, time set apart, private time, not public display time. You are one of His kids. Hold your head up, slightly bowed, absent of arrogance, but with your sincere request or your simple adoration and submission".

At the close of your day, the one thing that attracts the attention of our Creators' graces, above all the eloquent educated speeches offered, is a simple <u>thank you</u> even if at the moment the sincerity may be absent, He still dispenses His higher graces to reveal His presence to you even if you cannot feel them at that moment, be patient, or become a patient. I know this from direct experience by its practice and not from intellectual indulgences given by books. However I do read books for what to do, not for intellectual satisfactions only so I can sound off smartly from my arrogant base called my ego. Reading is an important form of studies, and a form of mental prayer as well.

Why the absolutes?

Why are they so offensive?

The absolutes are a cheese grater and we are the cheese.

When our ego's (the cheese) and arrogance rub up against the absolutes (the grater), we lose some hide, some of our precious ego is removed and it hurts our pride. When the ego is reduced, then there is more room for the considerations of others, and actions are now taken on behalf of others. And the promotion of the common welfare becomes our first consideration.

These *laws,* the absolutes, are non-flexible; however, we must be in order to become unyielding and non-flexible in our practice, by grace. When we are not flexible, we lose the art of saying "I was wrong" or "I'm sorry" and meaning it, thereby changing our behavior and becoming closer to our created essence, transforming us into those who, now possess the ability to stand firm on those principles, which are spiritual in their nature, moral in their humanity.

Thus, seeing how we are not absolutes, the targets are the absolutes, and we the people of the United States, should try to "form a more perfect Union."

And the word "sin" means to miss the mark. This does not mean that a sinner is a bad guy or gal. What's the target? The absolutes! Now we really get a sense of our own powerlessness and our need for and our dependency on a power greater than ourselves, <u>namely God</u>. It's not humiliating. It's *humbling*. So, if you have a problem with God, then you have a problem.

The following are some of the notes that I took in 1974 during some meetings with my mentor while he was sharing some of his experiences with prayer, which later I began to practice as an experiment as well.

The practical life means practice. I can teach a parrot to say anything, even quote scripture most perfectly, although the difference between a parrot and a patriot is that the parrot cannot do any of it, and the patriot *must* do it. It's his duty.

Prayer has two levels. The first is prayer of attention, and the second is prayer of grace.

1st: The prayer of attention takes two forms; both of which (A & B) are within our initiative and control as an act of the will of Man:

- A. Vocal Prayers: Talking with God. This is petition prayer which is low prayer: Next would be Intercession prayer which is middle prayer. Then next would be Thanksgiving prayers which are spoken group prayers; Sung prayer; Liturgical – Congregational prayer; Spoken repetition prayer.
- B. Mental Prayer: Meditation – Quiet Prayer; Attention to the Mind of God. Unspoken repetition of the Name.

2nd: The Prayer of Grace are of two forms: both of which (C & D) are NOT within our control or initiative, however, they can be experienced. [Personal Note: I have seen individuals experiencing the "C" type in some form or another, which is spontaneous and uncontrollable by the individual; gentle, and warm, with tears, not beyond the capacity of the individuals who are receiving this High Grace to endure, and they do not even know who is sending it because of His anonymity. Oh, the "Anonymity is the Spiritual foundation of the *laws*", ever reminding us to place Principles (*laws*) before personalities, doing our good works for the love of doing them and not just for the rewards (monies, or payoffs)]. I too have experienced this type of Grace.

C. Cordial Prayer offers: Preternatural clarity and truth, warmth, joy, rapture, bliss, unction, tears, fire, ecstasy, Bhakti, The Love of God, Compassion (leading to) service, (leading to) sacrifice. Prayer of the Heart: Repetition of the Name in the Heart.

D. Transcendental Prayer offers: Direct realization of God. Living Light. Literally beyond all description.

A personal observation is in order here, because, I too, have experienced the "C" type prayer, and it brought the tears and compassion. These were not tears of grief, or of pain, or of any wrong doings. These were like the tears of Mr. Beck, on national television, a man who has been ridiculed for expressing these tears given spontaneously by grace, ones not induced by an act of his own volition or initiative, but because of his compassion which has lead him to service and sacrifice for which he is so deeply grateful. Another would be Mr. Boehner who teared up during a speech, experiencing the tears of grace as a result of his compassion which has led him to service and led him to sacrifice for Our One Nation under God. This just personally reassures me that God is with us, dwelling among us, still dispensing His graces most anonymously. If I ever need a heart transplant, I'll take one of the ridiculers', not Beck's or Boehner's, because the ridiculers have never used theirs, and I personally have had nine heart attacks, four surgeries, and five stents beginning back in 2000. The gate at the marble orchard, as far as I was concerned, had closed, chain wrapped around it; however, someone forgot to lock it, because I'm still here and okay and the Angel of Death was not sent to retrieve my soul yet. I don't have a clue why. If I did have a clue, I would most probably wet my pants. So I will continue to live my life one day at a time, asking for knowledge of His Will and the Power to carry it out. No one can live in the morrow, it has not arrived yet. I too have experienced the tears of grace in front of others because of my personal gratitude, and I am not ashamed of them, for I <u>know</u> who sends them. "Ah, the tears, the tears", as my mentor would always say. Grown men weep in His Presence, realizing His goodness.

Thomas Merton said "*Compassion* is a keen awareness of the interdependence of all things.

Apparently, compassion does not mean to let murderers or those who blow up planes and kill others go free.

Many of the so-called mental illnesses of modern life are not mental illnesses at all. They are actually *Spiritual* illnesses, and they can be cured by switching from self-centered to God-centered living. But that switch is no small thing. It is a complete turnabout at the deepest center of a person's being, a profound alteration and relocation that has traditionally been called "Surrender".

Therefore, Surrender is our only option. Surrender to His Will by practicing, the four absolutes with a firm reliance on divine providence yields outcome to God.

This form of surrender has nothing to do with giving up our sword like Lee at Appomattox.

We must keep our swords, like the USS GEORGE WASHINGTON (one hell of a sword), for defending against the practitioners of deliberate and enjoyable evil. We are to protect ourselves and our allies. George Washington would have really enjoyed heating and air conditioning with ample food on his boat going forward, like we have today, not to participate in an act of deliberate and enjoyable evil but to defend himself and others against that evil and to promote liberty and justice and reluctantly do what was necessary for the preservation of that liberty and justice, not forcing it on anyone, only defending.

Lucifer created *nothing.*

Creation was done by this time! He did not even create himself. He voluntarily chose to go to that which had already been created by the one who has all power. Lucifer only has a silver tongue, no wetsuit to go swimming in. Lucifer is real enough and has had millennia of practice and knows all the tricks. He is such a good talker, influencing the soul via thought, convincing you or others that he is all that and a bag of chips. He didn't create his own kingdom! He chose it for a residence. We cannot out think him, and this is why we ask for God's protection and care with complete abandon to his divine providence each day.

Lucifer has only that power which is given him from above. Check out Job's story in the Good Book if you need more evidence.

We as individuals chose sides: We ask our Creator for His protection and care with complete abandon, while firmly relying on His divine providence by way of following His way of life, which is honest, pure, unselfish, and loving, attempting to live worthily while in His Presence, while receiving His blessings, even in our unworthiness.

It might be a good idea to attempt to change some of the unworthy practices we have when we observed them either individually or collectively as a nation.

The ability to observe in part some of our unworthiness is a gift. When revealed, it's never more than we can handle at any one time, and what we choose to do with that knowledge is up to us.

In reality, there are only three types of life styles;

1. God Centered Living

2. Diva Centered Living
3. Devil Centered Living

We live as citizens in one nation under God. Our founders laid the cornerstone (keystone) that supports our nation, one in which we can all walk as free men and women. A keystone is a stone that holds up the arch of a doorway through which all can pass through.

The <u>keystone</u> is The Way of the Grail.

The Way of the Grail is the Way for the men and women of this eon. It is the axis on which the material and spiritual evolution of the human race rests, and on which our great nation turns. It is the path of the present age, which includes the wisdoms and praxis of all ages.

The Way of the Grail is very high, deep, and special, but at the same time it is common, vulgar, and inescapable. It falls on every man and woman. It falls on you, whether you know it or not. You may already be actively involved in the Way of the Grail and not know it. If you honor the truth and serve it, if you love the good and seek it, trying, however humbly to be a real human being, you are on the path. Whether *you* can *stay* on the path and *grow* on it and *succeed* on it depends on your courage (guts) and fidelity (devotion). The guts referred to here have to be grown. No one is born with spiritual guts. On a d*aily* basis, one *must* remember the goal of practicing honesty, purity, unselfishness, and love. It is your capacity for knighthood. Don't let the word "knighthood" put you off. It just means that you must hang on to what you know is true and right, and live your life that way, without quitting or selling out. If you do that much, the Way will meet you, lead you, and support you.

The Way of the Grail is Christ-initiated, Christ-meditated, and Christ-centered, and it embraces all true ways. It never has been, is not now, and never can be a property of sectarians and bigots. The Way of Christ is catholic, i.e., inclusive and universal. It is the meeting place and melting pot of all the hopes, all the faiths, all the wisdom, all the energy and all the aspiration of all of mankind. [Note: The United States of America (an environment)(One Nation Under God) is the meeting place and melting pot of all the hopes, all the faiths, all the wisdom, all the energy and all the aspiration of all of mankind]. Note also that forgiveness is the ministry of Christ – should you do or bring harm to me, I forgive you which is non-retaliation and non-violent. That does not mean you can continue your degenerative practices in my presence or in my home sweet home or for me to continue to fellowship with you and let you keep harming me. If you want what I have, peace, then you must stop being violent and being a degenerative practitioner and become gentle. You must first learn to govern yourself. Should you choose otherwise, welcome to the many bar hotel for a "long, long, ---long, long, long ---long--------long time". (Thanks, Harrison Ford – his lines in the movie "Six days and Seven Nights")

Recall for a moment *who Christ is,* and you will see that it must be so.

He whom the Persians worshipped as Ahura Mazdao – he whom the Egyptians worshipped as Osiris and Pymander – he whom the Chinese worship as Teh and Tao – he whom the Hindus worship as Sat and Atman and

Vishnu and Ishvara – he whom the Buddhists worship as Tathata and Tathagata and the Dharmakaya – he whom the Muslims worship as al Hagg and Allah – he whom the Hebrews worship as Aehyeh and Jehovah – *he* is the one true God. And *he* is the one who has descended to mankind. There are not several of him; there is only one; there *can be* only one. And he now dwells in the earth in an essence which makes him both accessible and unavoidable. He has penetrated the planet to its core. He has infiltrated our land to its very rocks and trees, in a final campaign to rid it of its enemies once and for all.

The modern world is blinded by its immersion in materialistic illusions; however, even as men grope in unprecedented psychic darkness, the real destiny of our race unfolds, and we all – comprehending or uncomprehending – play our parts.

A great separation is taking place, and a great war is in progress – not one of our futile political or religious wars, with miserable egotistical ends in view, but a cosmic battle between Principalities and Powers – between Sons of Light and Sons of Darkness – with the fate of humanity and of every single human being hanging in the balance. In this struggle there are no bystanders. We are all combatants. The only questions are, do you realize what is happening? And whose side are *you* on.

In the midst of this world-wide convulsion of humanity – the Quest of the Grail – must now proceed. These conditions are not a hindrance to the Quest. On the contrary, they constitute the necessary matrix in which alone the Great Work can be brought to its term.

The end of the Quest is the encounter with the *substantial reality* of God – spiritual *and* material – supernatural *and* natural – immense *and* immediate – divine *and* human. The goal of this Way is the meeting with Emmanuel, God with us – the Son of the living God in that radiant form which can be seen, touched, tasted, consumed, and assimilated – to our everlasting sustenance, health and joy. [Note: The eye on top of the pyramid on our one dollar bill currency; our spiritual eye.]

The trouble is that the way seems too much. Nevertheless we are built for this quest and cannot live sanely without it. All attempts to defy it or escape it are doomed to endless frustrations. The love of God is, finally, inexorable: As Jeremy Taylor said: He threatens terrible things if we will not be happy.

I have discovered the above for myself, by grace. I cannot discover the truth of this for you. You will have to discover it for yourself.

Do not take my word for anything. Do your own homework. Perform your own experiment.

What are some of the Precepts of Christ that we as individuals and as a Nation are to attempt to do without defying them or escape our responsibility to perform? How about – change your attitude, your outlook, your way of life, your mind; go beyond your present state, transcend yourself (Greek *metanoia: meta,* "change" or "beyond"; *nous,* "intellect," "mind" "understanding"); or Wake up, Snap out of it. Pay attention. Watch (Greek *gregoreite).* Remember His time in the garden when He prayed and later found his disciples asleep asking them "could you not even watch with me for one hour"? How about being meek (Greek *praos,* "disciplined," like Regan – holding the course; "trained," "non-resentful," "gentle," "tractable," "teachable."; or how about the <u>biggie:</u> Be perfect (Greek *teleios,* "complete," "undivided," "unlimited," finished," "mature," "integral,") as God is perfect. What about Believe and trust in God as your Father, hallow his name, seek his kingdom and his truth, ask him for what you need, knock at the door of God (divine) realization.

The Greek words used above are the words used in the Greek translation of the New Testament, not meant to confuse anyone, and our equivalent meanings to their words.

Well, the argument against the forgoing will be that "we are not saints" or that "we are not perfect" which is a given, but a real – cop out – like, "we can continue to spend some monies we don't have and it's okay because "we are not perfect" – cop out (lying), or "we need more laws" – cop out (lying), or "we need to think this thru" – cop out (lying), or "we need to purchase some more friends by giving them monies" – cop out (lying). Look at all the dishonesty (lying) to ourselves and others. We are such ferocious liars, mostly to ourselves with so few truth tellers who have developed the Spiritual guts mentioned in the forgoing. Another example of lying (dishonesty) are the Doctors lying about some illness for Teachers who are willing to lie about a non-existent illness to justify their actions in Wisconsin, and neither the Doctors or the Teachers if asked if they are liars would say no we are not liars, we are honest citizens, yet justifying lying. There is the Absolute Honesty principle about simply no falsehood being betrayed. Both parties willing to lie to improve their personal positions (cop out – lying); having no spiritual guts or attempting to grow any spiritual guts at that moment in that opportunity presenting its self for growing some real guts. Opportunity knocks once where as temptations (to lie or cheat) beat on the front door forever (each tick of the clock). The simple solution is; *stop lying or cheating*. The simple solution is; *stop spending*. No wonder our children grow up confused, being told not to lie, yet seeing nothing but lying examples to follow then believing it's okay to lie. That's called teaching by example. It is easier to preach ten sermons than it is to live one sermon, requiring attention. This is called growing a conscience which is weak at birth (unconscious) and needs strengthening (becoming conscious) in adulthood. Remember, dishonesty is a degenerative principle and we suck ourselves down into the vortices of those degenerative practices which I mentioned in my other book "*Reclaiming National Sanity*". The last thing we want to give up is our suffering – the lying to ourselves and others – because we are so identified with the suffering, or if you will, our lying practices that were learned. God does not call the qualified – He qualifies the called, therefore the question is the following: Do you want to be a saint? Every saint has a past which only means that every sinner has a future and the common thread running through all the saints [Ancient and Modern; regardless of their warts or flaws] is that they only prayed for Knowledge of His Will and the Power to carry it out given their individual situations. Remember the word "sin" means to miss the mark, not that you are a bad person. Now we need His help to hit the mark. He can and will show us the way when we simply ask, giving Him credit for any successes we may have through His graces (powers); therefore the Will of God will never take you where the grace (power) of God will not protect you.

Strength relates to faith, and faith is the power to contact the truth. We currently are to recognize and accept the truth [like our current national dilemma – a nation being run by individuals seeking power – rather than our one nation under God.] We should trust and follow the truth even when it is not yet perceptually evident or logically demonstrable. However, right now, our national dilemma is perceptually evident and logically demonstrable. Faith, even at the ordinary levels of living, is directly and very practically related to strength. Why? Peter (faith) is the brother of Andrew (strength). When strength is low, then faith is low as well. Faith is a homing instinct for the truth we can sense in our guts, an instinct that transcends the sensual and rational functions. Spiritual faith is less common. Ordinary faith keeps us sane; spiritual faith leads us to peace and fulfillment. Ordinary faith illuminates ordinary life and keeps us from falling below the level of God's minimum intention for us, which helps us avoid becoming morally rotten or go crazy. Spiritual faith leads toward God's maximum intention for us, of which we see a forecast in the life of Christ Jesus. With a sound mind faith and reason complement and correct and stimulate each other. Let the steel of reason strike sparks from the rock of faith. Let them encourage and support each other, as in the lovely, sane words of the old hymn: "Faith, our outward sense befriending, make our inward vision clear".

Above all, faith is the power to trust the truth, to bet our lives on it, to leave all and follow it. (The letting go of old ideas absolutely.)

Our current national truth is, we're broke, and we need to go in the opposite direction, like – no free lunch – no more spending – the "a penny saved is a penny earned" Franklin thing.

Remember, "blind faith" is a contradiction in terms; there is no such thing; Blind belief, yes, but never blind faith.

We have now been experiencing a whole lot of blind beliefs – like promises made but never kept. Maybe the persons making the promises don't have the power they think they do. Is the universe tapping us on the shoulder *again*? Maybe we need to switch powers and placing our spiritual faith in the truth and trust God; You decide. You must choose.

I personally think it's about time that we the people become stronger Spiritual Patriots as well as American Patriots. In my experience, both are needed. Do your own homework! Don't take any of my word for it. Perform the experiment for yourself.

The uses and abuses of Anonymity

Anonymity takes on one of three different forms:
Anonymity is a spiritual foundation for spiritual progress, but in which direction.

First: <u>anonymity of inferiority</u> is not at all difficult to cultivate. Anyone doing something he or she is ashamed of naturally experiences a desire to be anonymous with regard to that piece of misbehavior. It can and frequently does, serve as a cover for lawlessness and violence. Robbers, looters, terrorists, rapists, and murderers often wear masks, or otherwise seek to avoid identification, in order to escape the just punishment of their destructive actions. Anonymity of this stripe is obviously an offense against humanity, and there is nothing to be said in its favor.

Second: <u>anonymity of mediocrity</u> has no such potential for evil, but neither is there anything to recommend it in a positive way. These are those whose lives are the medium, neither for much good nor for much evil, and are generally destined to live and die unknown outside their immediate circle of family and friends.

Third: <u>anonymity of excellence</u> is a rare and precious option, a blissful state known only by those in whom extraordinarily good things have come to pass, and who have elected to fore-go the personal recognition they would have every right to expect by ordinary worldly reckoning. It is the anonymity of excellence, and *only* this particular type of anonymity, which has the power (grace) to consecrate people's lives. This highest form of anonymity is a priceless part of our heritage.

In my view, this has a significant place within the framework of Spiritual in its nature, moral in its humanity, or spiritual in its nature, immoral in its humanity. Thusly the question is; which side are *you* on? – observe, then *choose.* Remember, one part body, two parts spirit! This sure seems like spiritual in its nature to me and even includes the practitioners of preachercraft, being those who hold others back by scandalizing others to make them feel bad or less than (small), preaching at them only trying to make themselves look good or better than others. Remember that judgment based on principles is <u>not</u> being judgmental.

Our Shining City on the Hill ain't so bright right now. WHY?

Firstly, we as individuals and as a Nation have distanced ourselves from the Absolutes mentioned earlier. In my earlier statement of "it is the way the Universe works, and it is the way you work, when you are in your right mind" refers to star brightness. All stars pulsate – how the universe works; All human hearts pulsate – how you work when you are in your right mind; Both having a rhythmic harmony in relation one to another. The heavens, stars, follow the absolute laws of brightness; whereas humans follow the absolute laws of honesty, purity, unselfishness, and love. The closer we as humans follow the laws of the Absolute (honesty, purity, unselfishness, love) the brighter our radiance and attractiveness or, if you will, awe in relation to others and the awe of the heavenly. The heavens display their radiance automatically, whereas we as humans have to choose it. The Universe expands the same as our Nation expands. The Universe is egoless, whereas our Nation has lots of egos which need to be kept in check via the Absolutes (the cheese grater); thusly the Macro and the Micro, both based upon *laws;* the longer the light period, the greater the Absolute magnitude or brightness of each star; thusly our shining city on the hill, which in truth, is His hill.

The Absolute (hottest – blue – 30,000 degrees k); then BW (blue white); then W (white); then YW (yellow white); then Y (yellow – the sun – 5,000 to 6,000 degrees k); then O (orange); then R (red – 3,000 degrees k – the coolest); therefore the *laws* of the Absolute are non-negotiable, dogmatic, unchanging, and unyielding regarding brightness; thusly the further we distance ourselves from the Absolute *laws* reflected in the heavens by our distancing ourselves from the Absolute *laws* – (Christ) – given mankind (honesty, purity, unselfishness, love), the lesser the magnitude of our brightness – the shining city on the hill – our One Nation Under God, the good. Again, the Heavens reflect brightness automatically (heavenly wisdom) because the heavens have no will – we as human beings *must choose* to return or change our direction by returning to the practice of the Absolutes of honesty, purity, unselfishness, and love as best we can – *daily* – then the morrow will reflect our renewed magnitude of brightness and the morrow within our bones shall be strengthened. As there are different star classes that pulsate, there are likewise human heart classes that pulsate. The brightest star in the Heavens – seen by all – the birth of the Absolute in living flesh (Christ) – descending to mankind showing men how to live – thusly all other stars pale in comparison and likewise all human hearts pale in comparison to the heart of the Absolute because of our choice to distance ourselves from honesty, purity, unselfishness, and love as individuals and as a nation; thusly diminishing our magnitude of brightness because of our chosen distance from the Absolute (Christ); the executive and sovereign monarch on our one nation and the universe – One Nation Under God, the good. The Absolutes are the yardstick by which spiritual progress is measured because we as individuals have a will – the brighter the glow within the heart, the warmer, lighter, and more gentle the heart.

Learning to navigate life using the absolutes as your instrument panel is like an aviator learning to become an instrument certified (IFR rated) pilot to navigate the skies (heavens) without being able to see any points of reference or even being able to see outside the cockpit and therefore must trust the instruments in front of him, disregarding his senses and trusting in the instruments only. I know this because of the degrees of difficulties and almost quit three times before I finally acquired my IFR certifications which have to be practiced daily in order to be proficient. Learning this art never promised a smooth flight, only a safe landing. Our Creator (God) never promised a smooth flight by practicing the absolutes and becoming proficient with their use while navigating through life, just a safe landing when we reach the marble orchard.

What profit has a man for all his labor under the Sun? One generation passes away and another generation comes – but the earth abides forever; the sun also rises and the sun also goes down – then hastens back to the place where it rose.

Don't you think it is now time to hasten back to our source "one nation under God" by practicing the four absolutes daily, returning to our absolute brightness as closely as humanly possible, unyieldingly? The *laws* are *dogmatic*! It appears to be unwise to put a question mark where our Creator has put a period. It appears Charlie Sheen is becoming a basket case and is not becoming a Moses. Moses started out as a basket case, literally; but Moses wanted to know the very existence of God, and found Him by simply seeking and asking.

Scientific Method

1. <u>Observation:</u> The harmony contained within the Universe.
2. <u>Hypothesis:</u> Are we really connected to the Spirit of the Universe?
3. <u>Prediction:</u> By using the hypothesis – make a prediction (yes or no)
4. <u>Test</u> the prediction: By experimentation (using the Four Absolutes, which are laws, as a base) and modifying the hypothesis by the results obtained.
5. Repeat 4 and 5 until there is no discrepancies between hypothesis and observation.

I have only tried to share what I now *know* and believe, and why my beliefs and actions have changed as a result of those who have taught me. This is my attempt to pass that knowledge on to you, even though I am no communicator, no writer, no minister, and a most unprofitable servant.

One last story: A mother was having a baby, and after the infant was delivered, the parents were given a heads up that things were unsafe to stay where they were, so the Foster father gathered his wife and infant together and left town. Now crossing desolate land to a new location and being extremely exhausted, they came upon a band of thieves. The leader of this band of thieves told others to leave these individuals alone and give to them shelter but he did not know why but sensed these individuals were somehow different. Later, the Mother of the infant needed water to give her infant his bath and requested some water for that purpose. A mother of a 3 year old boy brought water for her to bath her infant in and sensed there was something different about these individuals. After the infants' bath was finished, the mother of the 3 year old boy came to take away the used water and asked if she could use the water to bathe her 3 year old boy in. The Mother of the infant said yes and when the 3 year old boy, whose face was eat up with leprosy, was placed into the water, the leprosy was instantly healed and the 3 year olds' skin was now perfectly smooth and the water which was used to bath both boys was now still as pure as it was after the first bath was given. The mother of the 3 year old boy wanted to hold the infant who first bathed in the water but the Mother and Foster father said no but thanked them for the water and the next day left for their destination. Thirty some years later, this same infant child, followed by His Mother and Foster father, was taken and placed high on a hill after being whipped and cut by mankind, dying, for the whole and all of mankind and being placed between two thieves. The thief on His left was the same thief who bathed in His bath water and asked for Him to remember him when He enters into His Kingdom.

Have you been whipping and cutting anyone today, in actions, word, or thought? One might swallow a jigger of truth and hand out a cup of kindness, being a little meeker, and helping someone who is a little weaker.

In my previous book "*Reclaiming National Sanity*" I mentioned a portrait drawn by William Blake. Some of Blake's works are in our museums in Washington. Blake was a running buddy with Thomas Payne back in England, and Blake helped Payne escape into France so he would not be taken. Blake admired Washington and Franklyn and what they were doing in America. These were spiritually awake individuals and inspired by the spirit, not by bucks (monies). What's inspiring *you*? Is it the *Spirit* or the spirits of monies and/or the drugs? You decide.

Our nation is about what each individual can put into the stream of life, not what one can take out of the stream.

As for my personal belief or for anyone becoming our nations leader; First things First:

1. Homeland Security Leader: You have 7 days to have our southern borders reinforced with man power and old yellow school buses to take the illegal's back from wince they came or you're fired and our leader will find someone who can; with orders to warn violators to halt, with orders not to fire at violators unless fired upon and warn violators that if the violators are stupid enough to follow one of their "buddies" who will use weapons against us, the ensuing results will be brought upon themselves by an act of their own volition which was to choose to follow them. If you wish to become a Citizen, use the front door and register your intent for that purpose. Our riding companions are not The Four Horsemen of Conquest, War, Famine, or Death and we do not fear them or those who ride with them.

2. Since this is One Nation under God (Christ), who is the exemplar of the foundation of our nation, owning no possessions, then Our Government will release all lands and rights to usage of those lands

back to the States with no strings attached; not to include our established National Park lands or burial grounds and hopefully the States will allow cultivation of those lands by the citizens with rights to those properties if they can get those lands to produce. Not unlike the Sooner Land rush. This is getting back to "if you don't work, you don't eat" principle. Citizens may have possessions, but the Government may not have possessions.

3. A flat sales tax which includes everyone and the illegal's not yet discovered. No IRS forms anymore.

4. No more governmental bail outs, none; even the purchasing of "friends" in foreign lands. If the government gives monies, there will be no strings attached to those monies.

5. Put the spurs back on the Texas Rangers origination which I think were removed by a Kennedy and Conley agreement and reverse that order, giving back the Texas Rangers their grit so they can mount up and sink spur, One Riot, One Ranger, One Cartel, One Ranger, with reciprocity to and from neighboring states should they need assistance for the protection of our borders and her citizens as well. The Rangers never participated in acts of deliberate and enjoyable evil, only to defend our citizens from those who do participate and promote deliberate and enjoyable evil acts for self gain purposes.

6. A prayer chapel to be built on Capital grounds for prayer and meditation for those who would wish to attend with a secured entrance only because

of our current dilemma of evil practitioners. It would be great if our Congress men and women would use this chapel each morning prior to going to work. That is strictly voluntary. The President should set the example and lead services each morning or attend each morning prior to going to work in behalf of We the People. Remember, we have a daily reprieve based upon the maintenance of our Spiritual condition. That means practice. This small Chapel (facing east) to be built voluntarily by the contributions of materials and individuals having the God given skills, coming from their hearts and a small portion of their time (life) which is God given as well. No monies will be accepted for this purpose. No monies will be given for this purpose.

7. Unions, or any other contributors to governmental funds, those funds will be accepted, however, the contributors will receive no special considerations or favors of any kind or a seat at the table.

8. The United States of America – One Nation under God – Indivisible; will make a decision to place Honesty, Purity, Unselfishness, and Love (Christ) back at the head of the table, His earned and rightful place; thusly placing ourselves as servants and practitioners, which is our rightful place and duty, by voluntarily immersing ourselves in that purity thereby healing our whole body.

So, America, How Do You Like Your Tea?

WEAK – MEDIUM – STRONG

WEAK honesty etc., produces no change
MEDIUM honesty etc., not so safe, not so sure
STRONG honesty etc., produces positive changes in
those areas where applied every time.

Now, I'm going back into the woods to enjoy the peace
and serenity of the countryside where the silence and
calmness is so loud that unless one is accustomed to it, it
would seem unbearable, where there is only one way in
and one way out.